The Picture Perfect Pitcher

Tom House

Paul Reddick

ISBN: 1-58518-602-3
Library of Congress Control Number: 2001098601

Book layout: Jennifer Bokelmann
Diagrams: Chris Conlee
Cover design: Kerry Hartjen
Front cover photo: Ezra Shaw/Allsport

Coaches Choice
P.O. Box 1828
Monterey, CA 93942
www.coacheschoice.com

Dedication

To all those coaches who want to look at pitchers properly.

— Tom House

I would like to dedicate this book to the following people.

My wife, Stephanie. I love you and appreciate all of your loving help. Nothing that I have done would have happened without you.

My mother, Kathleen Reddick, Ed.D. You have been an inspiration of perseverance, pride, respect, dedication, love, and education. Thank you for being everything you are and more.

Bill, Kim, Ragen, and Avery Reddick. You have been everything to me.

And a special thanks to all my friends: Jack Byrnes, Rich Biddulph, Tom Clarke, Tim Clarke, Steve Grote, Bob Catullo, Brian Chapman, Dan Mondelli, Ray Korn, Bryan Malko, Corey Smith, Jim Reagan, Jr. and Sr., Rocky Letteiri, Yogi Berra, Dave Kaplan, Shoenhous and Shumko, Mollie Hopkins, Linda Hull, and most of all, Tom House—thanks for the education of a lifetime.

— Paul Reddick

Acknowledgments

Thanks to these pitchers for their pictures and to Bio-Kinetics for analyzing and teaching us what we are looking at.

— Tom House

Contents

Introduction

For over a century, pitching coaches, pitchers, medical professionals, and biomechanists have all searched for answers to one of baseball's most debated questions: What is a good pitching delivery?

Some very smart researchers from each of the preceding professions have come up with some great information and opinions about what makes up a good pitching delivery. Some of the opinions make sense, but most of what is thought and taught does not work or is presented in a way that does not make sense to coaches or athletes. Now, thanks to better information, improvements in technology, smarter instructional applications, and a synergy of off-the-field researchers and on-the-field instructors, anyone can confidently answer that question objectively and provide everyday applications for coaches and players.

Chapter 1 addresses conventional wisdom and misinformation. This will help to eliminate some of the bad pitching instructions that are out there.

In Chapter 2, you will learn the five absolutes of pitching a baseball. These absolutes represent what the healthy, successful pitchers in baseball do to throw. It is not a cookie cutter approach to pitching, having every pitcher look the same. The absolutes allow for stylistic interpretations and feel.

In Chapters 3 through 5, you will see detailed deliveries of 15 of the best pitchers of the recent past, present, and the stars of tomorrow, and also see how the five absolutes work for each pitcher despite their stylistic differences.

Unorthodox deliveries will be the focus of Chapter 6. You will see that sometimes what the eye sees is not what actually happens. In Chapter 7, you will see pictures of everyday players like Craig Biggio and Derek Jeter throwing just like pitchers. Throwing is throwing no matter where you are on the field.

In the appendix, Eric Bentley of Bio-Kinetics will show you the latest technology available to help you measure your skill and how you can see how you compare with the best in the game.

Taken in parts or as a whole, The Picture Perfect Pitcher will serve as a visual companion to the instructional information currently available and a definitive resource for objective analysis of pitching a baseball.

CHAPTER 1

A Picture is Worth a Thousand Words

As we traveled around the country and and the world, we worked with many different players and coaches. Although certain we had the best information and instruction available, we still failed with too many players. We started looking at how our instructional sessions were organized and for ways to improve them. We went back to the basics of teaching and asked ourselves: How do athletes learn?

What we found is that athletes learn by:

- Hearing
- Seeing
- Feeling

With this in mind, we reevaluated our instructional sessions. Most of the time spent during instruction was talking about mechanics (hearing) and doing drills for skill (feeling). Although we would demonstrate good mechanics (seeing), we spent very little time focusing on the visual aspect of learning.

We starting adding pictures of elite pitchers to our instructional sessions. The results were amazing. Pitchers were saying:

- "Oh, I finally get it."

- "Now I see what you mean."
- "That's what is looks like."

Once we had a breakthrough in communication, we were better able to match up a pitcher's style with that of an efficient major leaguer.

Misinformation

Experienced pitchers and pitching coaches recognize a good delivery when they see one, but for the most part they don't know what they are actually looking at. We informally asked 10 coaches and players from all levels what good pitching mechanics were.

The coaches said:

- "It depends on who you are talking about."
- "Being smooth and fluid."
- "Let me see them throw, and I'll tell you if there good."

The players said:

- "Big high kick, point the ball at second, throw over the top, and grab some dirt on the follow though."
- "My coach said Nolan Ryan had good mechanics."
- "You don't want to throw like El' Duque."

The answers are not very clear as to what a good delivery is, but they do represent the way most coaches and players think.

Conventional Wisdom

Conventional wisdom is opinion that has been repeated enough over time to become accepted as fact. While sometimes it can be fact, most times it is not. This is a sign of a significant problem for our contemporary game. Because baseball is very reluctant to go outside itself for expertise, conventional wisdom perpetuates itself. Intelligent, well-intentioned resources, front-office management, on-field mangers, coaches, players, scouts, and even media personalities on TV and radio who have become recognized as experts are all disseminating a lot of misinformation. The following is an example of the conventional wisdom that permeates baseball today.

Conventional Wisdom #1

Opinion: Do not land on your heel.

Objective Information: As long as you maintain balance and posture it doesn't matter how you land.

Illustration: Notice Eckersley, Maddux and Brown all landing on their heel.

Eckersley

Brown

Maddux

Conventional Wisdom #2

Opinion: Keep your foot under your knee for balance while lifting.

Objective Information: As long as you maintain dynamic balance (head over belly between the balls of your feet) with no head movement, it doesn't matter how you lift.

Illustration: Check out Ryan, Wagner, and Hoffman with their feet well outside of their knees.

Ryan

Wagner

Hoffman

Conventional Wisdom #3

Opinion: Point your toe down to lift.

Objective Information: As long as you maintain dynamic balance (head over belly between the balls of your feet) with no head movement, it doesn't matter how you lift.

Illustration: Notice Wood with his toe down, Pettitte with his toe up, and Martinez with his toe straight.

Ezra Shaw/Allsport

Dave Sandford/Getty Images

Martinez

Pettitte

Matthew Stockman/Allsport

Wood

Conventional Wisdom #4

Opinion: Drop and drive vs. tall and fall

Objective Information: Actually, neither is very good. A pitcher must find a consistent posture and keep a consistent posture.

Illustration: David Cone postures low but maintains that posture throughout his delivery. Randy Johnson postures tall and stays there.

Cone

Johnson

Conventional Wisdom #5

Opinion: Thumbs down to get elbows up.

Objective Information: Let the arm path happen. Simply match up the frontside with the backside in an opposite and equal-elbow alignment.

Illustration: Glavine, Cone, and Pettitte all have different arm slots with an opposite and equal frontside.

Cone

Glavine

Pettitte

Conventional Wisdom #6

Opinion: Don't throw across your body; point your toe.

Objective Information: You can only stride across your body the width of your hips with balance, posture, and late rotation. The shoulders will still square up over the front foot.

Illustration: Ryan and Clemens both stride across their body with a closed toe.

Jonathan Daniel/Allsport

Rick Stewart/Allsport

Ryan   **Clemens**

Conventional Wisdom #7

Opinion: Don't throw sidearm; get on top.

Objective Information: The arm path is genetic; let it happen.

Illustration: Eckersely, Martinez, and Maddux all have different arm slots.

Martinez

Eckersley

Maddux

Conventional Wisdom #8

Opinion: Pull the glove to the hip.

Objective Information: This is the difference between what the eyes see and what actually happens--all successful pitchers bring the body to the glove.

Illustration: Maddux, Brown, and Ryan all bring their bodies to the glove.

Maddux

Brown

Ryan

Conventional Wisdom #9

Opinion: Push off the rubber.

Objective Information: You can't push down a hill. All elite pitchers find a posture and keep a posture by stabilizing with their post leg.

Illustration: If Clemens or Martinez pushed off the rubber, their back legs would straighten out!

Clemens

Martinez

CHAPTER 2

Pitching Absolutes

Biomechancial Research

Over time with throwing workloads, pitchers are only as strong as their weakest link and only as efficient as their worst movement. On flat ground or on the mound, pitchers' weight transfers from back foot to front foot, creating energy that sequences through the body from the feet to the fingertips and out into the baseball.

Movement that is out of sequence, or any strength that is recruited out of sequence, will cause pitchers to suffer with performance problems or injury. The body is designed to work on flat ground. Pitching and throwing is not an unnatural movement. However, pitching off the mound is unnatural because the slope of the mound causes excess muscle and joint stress during weight transfer and sequential muscle/energy loading.

Pitchers are born with arm speed. The velocity of a pitch is determined by how their genetic ratio of fast-twitch/slow-twitch muscle fiber passes energy from their feet through their body and arm into the baseball. Body size and absolute strength have nothing to do with arm speed; it's genetics supported by functional strength and mechanical efficiency. Two of the hardest throwers and best pitchers in the game respectively, Billy Wagner and Pedro Martinez, are both less than six feet tall and weigh less than 200 pounds.

Motion analysis validates five biomechanical coaching imperatives. Everything else is a non-teach, inevitable, or unimportant.

Objective Information

Backed by the resources at Biokinetics, Inc., and the Functional Fitness Institute, Inc., we've captured pitching data, analyzed motions, examined strength protocols, tested metabolic management, tested tissue recovery, and evaluated coaching techniques from the Orient, Europe, Latin America, Australia, Canada, and the United States.

The database is large (in the thousands) and contains competitive deliveries of over 300 professional pitchers, analyzed for mechanical efficiency in three dimensions at shutter speeds of 1,000 frames per second. It has shown what the best do to pitch a baseball. Unfortunately, it's often not what the best in baseball teach. Statistically, baseball is a game of failure. The data reveals that most succeed in spite of the conventional wisdom surrounding them. The following will explain and expand on this phenomena.

Dynamic Balance

Dynamic Balance is defined as head over the center of gravity between the balls of the feet through weight transfer into the launch and throw. It creates an axis of rotation for the torso and arms when the head and the center of gravity track as far forward as functional strength and flexibility will allow. The ball of the foot/arch complex in a pitchers' feet provide the neurological input for the brain and the inner ear to help the body position itself properly during the kinetic delivery--what biomechanists call proprioception and kinesthetic awareness.

Dynamic Balance

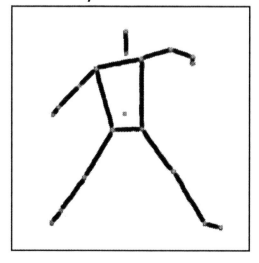

Postural Stabilization

Postural Stabilization is defined as keeping the head stable and parallel to the ground/mound from the leg lift to the launch. It directs the total body mass towards home plate during the weight transfer and the sequential muscle loading/energy release into the baseball.

Postural Stabilization

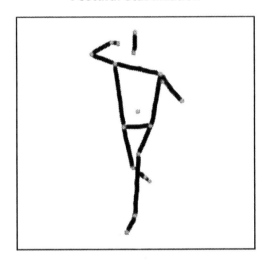

Equal-and-Opposite Elbow Alignment

The Equal-and-Opposite Elbow Alignment is defined as lining the elbows up while having the same forearm angles in both throwing and glove arms at the foot strike. It facilitates timing in the muscle/energy sequencing coming up the body. A properly positioned glove side sends a message of patience to the inner ear and minimizes the tendency for the frontside to spin out.

Equal-and-Opposite Elbow Alignment

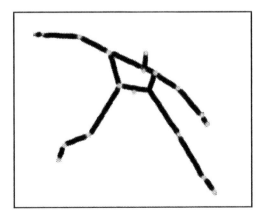

Late-Torso Rotation

Late-Torso Rotation is defined as the hips delaying any rotation until at least 75% of the stride length, with the shoulders rotating and squaring up towards home plate late over the ball of foot/arch of the landing foot. This positions the body's axis of rotation close to home plate as functional strength and flexibility will allow. It also minimizes stress on the throwing shoulder and elbow into the launch.

Late-Torso Rotation

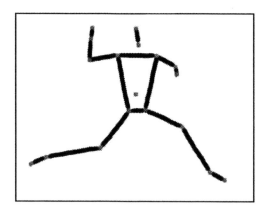

Blocking the Glove

Blocking the Glove is defined as keeping the glove and the elbow stationary and inside the width of the body during torso rotation into the launch. It keeps the weight transfer and muscle/energy sequencing directional while the upper body rotates and delivers the throwing arm and the baseball. Taking the body to the glove gets the release point closer to home plate. This means more strikes and less time for the hitter to see and read the pitch, later movement on all pitches as they approach the strike zone, and less stress on the arm.

Blocking the Glove

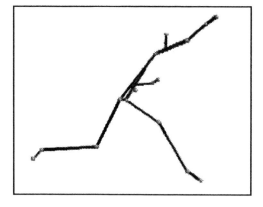

CHAPTER 3

Modern Day Legends

Roger Clemens

★

Nolan Ryan

★

Tom Seaver

★

Dennis Eckersley

Roger Clemens

What Is Unique: All Absolutes -- Clemens is perfect.

Years Played: 18

Average Innings Per Start: 7

K/BB Ratio: 3.5:1

Win/Loss: 260 - 142

Balance

Equal and Opposite Elbows

Late Rotation

Blocked-Off Frontside

Finish

Nolan Ryan

What Is Unique: Dynamic Balance -- Ryan had the ability to maintain dynamic balance with an extremely high lift that recruited more energy into his pitch.

Years Played: 27

Average Innings Per Start: 7

K/BB Ratio: 2:1

Win/Loss: 324 – 292

Balance

Equal and Opposite Elbows

Late Rotation

Blocked-Off Frontside

Finish

Tom Seaver

What Is Unique: Late Rotation -- Seaver rotated at close to 90% of his stride length.

Years Played: 20

Average Innings Per Start: 7 1/3

K/BB Ratio: 3:1

Win/Loss: 311 – 204

Balance

Equal and Opposite Elbows

©Bettman/Corbis

Late Rotation

Blocked-Off Frontside

Finish

Dennis Eckersley

What Is Unique: Postural Stabilization and Blocked-Off Frontside -- "Eck" keeps a firm, upright posture into a blocked-off frontside.

Years Played: 24

K/BB Ratio: 4:1

Win/Loss: 197 -171

Saves: 397

Balance

Equal and Opposite Elbows

Stephen Dunn/Allsport

Late Rotation

Stephen Dunn/Allsport

Blocked-Off Frontside

Craig Melvin/Allsport

Finish

CHAPTER 4

Current Superstars

Randy Johnson

Pedro Martinez

Greg Maddux

Tom Glavine

Kevin Brown

Randy Johnson

What Is Unique: Dynamic Balance and Postural Stabilization -- At 6'11", Johnson maintains perfect dynamic balance and postural stabilization throughout his delivery.

Years Played: 13

Average Innings Per Start: 7

K/BB Ratio: 3:1

Win/Loss: 179 - 95

Balance

Equal and Opposite Elbows

Ezra Shaw/Getty Images

Doug Pensinger/Allsport

Late Rotation   **Blocked-Off Frontside**

Ezra Shaw/Allsport

Finish

Pedro Martinez

What Is Unique: Speed of Delivery -- Martinez has a very live delivery. He goes at an amazing clip but maintains all absolutes.

Years Played: 9

Average Innings Per Start: 7

K/BB Ratio: 4.5:1

Win/Loss: 125 - 56

Balance

Equal and Opposite Elbows

Dave Sandford/Getty Images

Late Rotation

Al Bello/Getty Images

Blocked-Off Frontside

Peter J. Taylor/Allsport

Finish

Greg Maddux

What Is Unique: Late Rotation — Maddux rotates at 83% of his stride length. This means less stress, more strikes, and late movement.

Years Played: 15

Average Innings Per Start: 7

K/BB Ratio: 3:1

Win/Loss: 240 - 135

Balance

Equal and Opposite Elbows

Stephen Dunn/Allsport

Late Rotation

Jed Jacobsohn/Allsport

Blocked-Off Frontside

Andy Lyons/Getty Images

Finish

Tom Glavine

What Is Unique: Equal and Opposite Elbows, Late Rotation, and Blocked-Off Frontside — Glavine is as good as anyone who as ever pitched a baseball; just look at his efficiency.

Years Played: 14

Average Innings Per Start: 6 2/3

K/BB Ratio: 2:1

Win/Loss: 208 – 125

Balance

Equal and Opposite Elbows

Stephen Dunn/Allsport

Late Rotation

Jim Gund/Allsport

Blocked-Off Frontside

Jonathan Kirn/Allsport

Finish

Kevin Brown

What Is Unique: Equal and Opposite Elbows — Kevin maintains his elbow alignment until he has tracked to 75% of his stride length and his hips have completely turned towards home plate.

Years Played: 14

Average Innings Per Start: 7

K/BB Ratio: 2.5:1

Win/Loss: 170 –114

Balance

Equal and Opposite Elbows

Tom Hauck/Allsport

Late Rotation

Adam Pretty/Getty Images

Blocked-Off Frontside

Tom Hauck/Allsport

Finish

CHAPTER 5

Up and Coming:
The Stars of Tomorrow

Kerry Wood

★

Andy Pettitte

★

Billy Wagner

★

Mariano Rivera

★

Trevor Hoffman

Kerry Wood

What Is Unique: Equal and Opposite Elbows — Wood had perfect elbow alignment.

Years Played: 2

Average Innings Per Start: 6 2/3

K/BB Ratio: 3:1

Win/Loss: 20 −13

Balance

Equal and Opposite Elbows

Late Rotation

Blocked-Off Frontside

Finish

Andy Pettitte

What Is Unique: Equal and Opposite Elbows — Pettitte has a big tilt in his elbows but still maintains perfect alignment.

Years Played: 6

Average Innings Per Start: 6 2/3

K/BB Ratio: 2:1

Win/Loss: 100 – 55

Balance

Equal and Opposite Elbows

David Seelig/Allsport

Late Rotation

Jamie Squire/Allsport

Blocked-Off Frontside

David Seelig/Allsport

Finish

Billy Wagner

What Is Unique: Velocity — Wagner throws 99 mph and is only 5'11". He's a combination of genetics and perfect mechanics.

Years Played: 5

K/BB Ratio: 4:1

Saves: 107

Balance

Equal and Opposite Elbows

Late Rotation

Blocked-Off Frontside

Finish

Mariano Rivera

What Is Unique: Smoothness — Rivera maintains perfect mechanics with a smooth, slow tempo.

Years Played: 6

K/BB Ratio: 4:1.5

Saves: 165

Balance

Equal and Opposite Elbows

Jed Jacobsohn/Allsport

Late Rotation

Scott Halleran/Getty Images

Blocked-Off Frontside

Andy Lyons/Allsport

Finish

Trevor Hoffman

What Is Unique: Dynamic Balance — Hoffman is able to maintain dynamic balance with a high lift of his foot far outside of his knee.

Years Played: 8

K/BB Ratio: 3:1

Saves: 271

Balance

Equal and Opposite Elbows

Late Rotation

Blocked-Off Frontside

Finish

CHAPTER 6

A Little *Funky*: Unorthodox Deliveries

Orlando "El Duque" Hernandez

John Rocker

Hideo Nomo

Rob Nen

Orlando "El Duque" Hernandez

What Is Unique: Dynamic Balance — Hernandez does an excellent job of maintaining balance through an unorthodox delivery.

Years Played: 3

Average Innings Per Start: 6 2/3

K/BB Ratio: 2:1

Win/Loss: 41 - 26

Balance

Equal and Opposite Elbows

Jed Jacobsohn/Allsport

M. David Leeds/Getty Images

Late Rotation

Blocked-Off Frontside

David Seelig/Allsport

Finish

John Rocker

What Is Unique: All Absolutes — Rocker is herky jerky while maintaining all absolutes.

Years Played: 3

K/BB Ratio: 2:1

Saves: 64

Balance

Equal and Opposite Elbows

Andy Lyons/Allsport

Late Rotation

Ronald Martinez/Getty Images

Blocked-Off Frontside

Tom Pigeon/Allsport

Finish

Hideo Nomo

What Is Unique: The Tornado — Nomo twists, turns, rocks, and tilts, but maintains all absolutes while doing so.

Years Played: 6

Average Innings Per Start: 6 1/3

K/BB Ratio: 2:1

Win/Loss: 69 – 61

Balance

Equal and Opposite Elbows

Lisa Blumenfeld/Getty Images

Late Rotation

Stephen Dunn/Getty Images

Blocked-Off Frontside

Jeff Gross/Getty Images

Finish

Rob Nen

What Is Unique: "The Tap" Nen takes a normal lift but then taps his toes on the ground before moving towards home plate.

Win/Loss: 45-42

Saves: 314

ERA: 2.98

K/BB Ratio: 3:1

Balance

Equal and Opposite Elbows

Late Rotation

Blocked-Off Frontside

Finish

CHAPTER 7

Everyday Throwers

Nomar Garciaparra

★

Craig Biggio

★

Alex Rodriguez

★

Derek Jeter

★

Chipper Jones

★

Mike Piazza

Nomar Garciaparra

Ezra O. Shaw /Allsport

Equal and Opposite Elbows

Jeff Gross /Allsport

Blocked-Off Frontside

Craig Biggio

Jonathan Daniel/Allsport

Equal and Opposite Elbows

Harry How/Allsport

Blocked-Off Frontside

Alex Rodriguez

Tom Hauck/Getty Images

Blocked-Off Frontside

Otto Greule Jr./Allsport

Finish

Blocked-Off Frontside

Chipper Jones

Stephen Dunn/Allsport

Equal and Opposite Elbows

Brian Bahr/Allsport

Blocked-Off Frontside

Mike Piazza

Donald Miralle/Allsport

Equal and Opposite Elbows

Aubrey Washington/Allsport

Blocked-Off Frontside

See How You Match Up with the Pros

Bio-Kinetics

Bio-Kinetics is a San Diego-based, human performance organization. It was founded with one sole purpose in mind—to help athletes of all ages achieve their peak performance while keeping them injury free. In order to accomplish this goal, thousands of pitchers have been filmed, from the Major League level down to the Little League level, and their mechanics have been analyzed to come up with a model for what the most successful pitchers in the game do. After spending countless hours critiquing and measuring all aspects of the delivery on all the pitchers, it was discovered that all pitchers have certain mechanical aspects of their delivery that they must do in order to stay consistent and injury free. Bio-Kinetics has worked with the best pitchers in the game, including Nolan Ryan, Roger Clemens, Tom Glavine, and Randy Johnson. In the process, it has been discovered that whether the pitcher is a flame-throwing power pitcher or a soft-throwing crafty pitcher, their mechanics are all basically the same.

At Bio-Kinetics, the steps involved in undertaking a biomechanical analysis are relatively straightforward. First, a video is taken of an individual pitching in a game, or on the side during a bullpen. Then, that video of the player's mechanics is converted into a 3D stick figure image through a complicated process and the use of Bio-Kinetics' technical computer system. Once the player is in the computer as a 3D image, all aspects of his delivery can be measured with 100% accuracy, and he can be shown any imaginable angle of his mechanics to help illustrate and better understand a particular aspect of his performance. Among the aspects of a pitcher's motion that are measured are stride length, dynamic balance, postural stabilization, angle of forearms at foot landing, late rotation, and glove/glove elbow positioning. Once these measurements are obtained, Bio-Kinetics can then compare the individual to what the most mechanically efficient pitchers do, and see how he measures up.

With his analysis, each individual receives a three-page written assessment that identifies his mechanical problems and gives him solutions for how to overcome those problems. Bio-Kinetics also gives the individual a grade on Bio-Kinetics' mechanical-efficiency scale to give the athlete an idea as to where he is right now from a biomechanical standpoint, and how he compares to other pitchers at his level and at higher levels of ball. Furthermore, the athlete is given a detailed, but simple, plan as to how he can reach his personal best, and then the rest is up to him. Over the years, Bio-Kinetics has had many players come to them for an assessment who have, with hard work, dramatically improved their mechanics and their ability in a short period of time.

3-D motion analysis allows the pitcher to view his mechanics as compared to an elite professional. In the sample, an amateur's pitching mechanics (figure on right) are compared to that of Nolan Ryan (figure on left).

Notice in the first picture how the amateur has already changed posture after lift.

The amateur is starting to fly open while Nolan holds perfect elbow alignment.

As Nolan holds his elbows in place and glides to rotate late, the amateur starts to change posture to deliver the baseball.

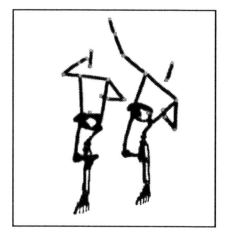

Nolan's posture is firm and stable, while the amateur continues to change posture and drag his elbow.

At release point, notice how much closer Nolan is to the plate.

After release, Nolan continues forward while the amateur falls off to the side.

ABOUT THE AUTHORS

Tom House is recognized as one of the world's foremost authorities on pitching. He pitched on the professional level from 1967 to 1979 for the Atlanta Braves, the Boston Red Sox, and the Seattle Mariners. He has coached since 1980 for the Houston Astros, San Diego Padres, Texas Rangers, and Chiba Lotte Marines (Tokyo). Fluent in Spanish, he has also coached in Latin America. On the amateur level, Tom is an information and instruction coordinator for 12 baseball academies across the United States and Canada. He directly accesses 8,000 to 10,000 players a year in clinic settings.

House is also a scientist and researcher. His company, Bio-Kinetics, leads the way in computerized, three-dimensional motion analysis, helping athletes learn how to maximize performance through proper biomechanics. Another of his companies, Functional Fitness Paradigms, trains elite and everyday athletes to optimize their physical strengths and flexibility.

House holds a Ph.D. in psychology. He travels the world as an international consultant, performance analyst, and sports psychologist.

Paul Reddick is one of the brightest young leaders in sports. Paul currently lectures youth around the country about sports violence and bullying. Paul has served as a professional scout for the Pittsburgh Pirates and as a state delegate for USA Baseball. In addition, Paul owns the New Jersey Baseball Academy. Paul has also served as a performance consultant to St. Barnabas Sports Medicine Institute and Health South Rehabilitation Center, and as a volunteer at The Yogi Berra Museum and learning center. Currently enrolled in the Life Learners program at Columbia University, Paul has also traveled extensively throughout Europe providing baseball and fitness consultations. Paul can be contacted at PaulReddick@aol.com.